India

Poems from here

Russell Buker

Copyright © 2019 *India* by Russell Buker

Published by Piscataqua Press
an imprint of RiverRun Bookstore
32 Daniel Street
Portsmouth NH 03801

ISBN: 978-1-950381-07-4

Contents

Heat-wave

those dogs in heaven
sleep
in later these days
gazing

far
into haze, infinite
variation
dawns on us, still

bashful
but not as though
feeling
abandoned-Aphelion

she
stops to smile as
windows
open for the breeze

movement
without mass un-
alloyed
drifted to far to

return
like the child on
the beach
no one will pick

up
her settlement
settled
even in her death

Left

I am left
on
glass-hot
sands

siphoning phonemes
written
by persons I
know

nothing about,
in
language foreign
Emily

going to miss,
would
you like to
listen

know how warm
vowels
can become
left

Raid

a raid on the in-
articulate
with shabby equip-
ment
always deteriorating
Sujatha Mathia

believing I'm
normal
floating on
angry
waters carrying
ballast

lonelier than any-
one
else, borrowing
fishing
lines afloat carrying
ballast

Nature only counts
if
man-made which is
politically
questioning carrying
ballast

while the sprouting
seeds
in ballast keep on
jumping
ship in every port
quietly

and epic storms that
sprout
and wave for whole
days
and nights do not
bother

one carrying ballast

Yes

these dreams bother
me,
morbid you always say,
but
more than if I am
asleep:

clouds rolling in as
earth
rolls over earth singing,
burning
drunken petals escape
dance

that will save them
surprised
in silken dust when
all
along we did think
crust

would finally remain
stable
until we were the
ones
responsible for our
extinction

morbid you say. OK
I
say do you think
your
god gives us a lava-
flow

Secret

friends land on
my
hand-little feet
on
my hand and
then
cocking its head
to
listen for the sounds
and
what for or since
when
does the fear of
success,
Alethia, obviate
fears
of failures hallucin-
ations
of rented thought
resting
its chin on granite
skin
approaching the gloomy,
ominous
before picking a seed
and
gleefully flying off into
darkness

Title

we are in the nickel,
dimes
part of the equation

probably
on the periphery
where

no cents reigns
and
too late for any old

home
welcoming with its
cut

stone entry granite,
no
door left to knock,

with
tiny Garnets that
light

up when moonlight
shifts
slowly down the lane

shining
red while all homeless
ghosts

watch thawed leaves in
the yard
awaken, come alive

were
is the house cat who
slept

certain all these lights
are
still warm at night

Should

I worry when our
magnetic
field flops over
what's
gained, lost: like
winds
that coursed
through
fragrant cedars
Lebanon's
finest boat building
wood
that only plies the
waters
left in my mind
next
to Teosinte, corn,
in
a hard-packed
Milpa,
fields, begging for
fragrant
winds, rain-drops,
shade
from stalled clouds
yes
and Aztec prayers

Eye

cry4 protein in their
eye
yet traveling birds are
not
as plentiful this
year
while bits of sun
still
warm flight feathers

return
as magnetic fields
weaken
getting ready to
flip
while wavering
black
coffee suffices for
now

God knows where it
ends
places lost in our past
that's
the difference between
fantasy,
reality sending them
to
new vanishing points

Dreams

The weight wondering
where
you spent the night in
dream
among Rosby waves
dark
then white just
before
dawn brings a wind's
strong
gusts to silence any
dream
that foretold what
tomorrow
should seem to be

open
hands add their
frustration
while sunlight drifts
through
fingers of wanna-be
soon
to flowered-bright
allows
a scent of that I
am
fearful of falling
with
blossoms silent sound

I know, I know ICU

who remembers who
woke
our mother and what
is
her life-span's soft
pity

where my thoughts
are
an unsolvable equation
as
whatsoever equals another
day

that creates her own
space
among heavy, greening
trees
while the hold- fast light
noon

argues with no one
even
cancer or dementia as
long
as its angle holds off
caring
softness of another night

Here we go

where only few remember and:
then
wind set down
every-
one else will drown
parts
part of the sea
as
godless men flee
slavery
to a stand on border
shooting
Palestinian fodder

Moses!!
what hath god wrought
killing
without much thought
Again!!
Moses' stone broken in sand

Prodding

days of flinching
prodding
Earle did not want to
come
to the marble graves
where
people stand to look
back

selfies grown colder in
weather
remind me to tell Earle
celluloid
used by our digital
cameras
emulate him as statue's
weathered

cheek resembles his birth-
mark
but no one listens as
when
I first saw you I said
hi
as we were of an equal
age

Back

back to the light again
as
if we never left with
quick
sealing surgical glue
to
keep the floor of
dour
down with the rest
along
with the bodies to
come

tuning and amplification,
lonesome
getting nearer, while the
trees
lose their sole grayness
after
the cruel winter clipped
warm
from their arms and
water
stilled its oxygen notes to
utterly

tongue-tied abrasion and
now

stare poems in their book-
ish
face sprouting along
with
greening pastels of
thought
surging with the burgeoning
water-
table past the hindering
doors

Tonight

I'm usually not one for starting
worry
but I am unsure what woke
me
last night at 2 AM: Put my
arm
up and it seemed to throb,
glow
as it had no distinct edges,
only
an ebb with a return especially
while
neuropathetic rivers of pain
run
along bottoms of one's
feet
only to subside swollen and
dangerous
as a 3 way bulb with its
middle
range flashed and gone
out
leaving one in the dark
alone
wondering why suddenly
I
fear for my soul lying
there,

it's the last place to
go
while the brain fights
loss
of oxygen everywhere but
puddled
indistinct orbited brainwaves

Energy

Oh stop one of
us
begs whatever
startled

you
restless in me
too
how is anyone to

know
when a nerve has
had
enough and voices

its,
our, vulnerability
as
those balloons

we
filled for birthdays
before
the candles were

lit
when their information
energy
and particles burst

our

world when one candle

grabbed

a balloon and we

reconnected

in the release of air

in

the party's middle

April Fools

let the privet
hedge
swing with wet
rampage
of fog and wind
grown
daring to mind
its
self out in blind
thrust
not a moment
too soon
leaving dark behind
leaving
with little regret

Arecebo

is the incubation period
over
all disk galaxies rotate
once
every billion years

1974's limelight message
slows
through M13's globular
cluster
without straining our

talent
resting on barren dust
where
for all practical purposes
our

static gold lie true as the
bias
of its receiver who is at the
age
who is at the age and

wondering
if we have eaten a pound
of
dirt or made everything
up

as we went along with

our

guesses and reconstructions

of

emotions generated during

space

changes in our bodily

state

Works

one longs to have done something
in the world -V. Woolf

even photons at work
stop
at their silent fade
of
vanishment to
space
waiting for time's
crinkle
to catch up so
they
may resume moving
away
from us well
after
moving through
our
static stance, lonely
ice-
bergs stop here too
before
steerage into open
waters
trained to go on
wanting
everything in the speed

lane
while music from
an
older parade bounds,
marries
the pineal horizon
where
no one waves
back

Same storm

no one saw this
happening
how can this
be:
anonymous and
with-
out usual strength
life-
less existence
an
athlete of small
muscles
failing instinct

what
type of cunning
was
this as my star
re-
filled with frost-laden
words
cooled metrics joy-
ously
gone as shovelfuls
of
snow long gone
melted

5:AM, March 2

the world turned
in-
voluntary as my
feet
clawed the wet
air
my hands fled down-
wards
in what I hoped was
more
stability as rain
when
it landed immediately
froze
to whatever was on
earth
as I slid away to
feed
the birds watching
from
what I think I remem-
bered
as well adjusted trees

Farewell

but
I told you a
dream's
the same as
vision

farewell my
favorite
lake that's
merely
temporary
with

free fishing
and
laundry, no
more
tears, no
more

tensile, you
crumble
as I walk while
dead
fish swim
grass-

less with salt
hearts
up during the
day-
tame that wild
blood

sugar now at
seven
from night noise
when
I have had mine
up

to 9 feeling
fine
with a vision of
man
diving into wet
hole

in dried lake bed
fare-
well, fare the
well

Stories in carbon

were you telling
me
which to prefer
I
can barely make
you
out in the smokey
light
of the cave and
your
long hair makes
for
a sexless outline
as
you drew quick
lines
of the animal you
are
intoning hunger
to
the spirit of the
animal
we are not sup-
posed
to sing as our
many
brain disorders
are not

from imbalances
of
atmospheric CO2's
but
brain disorders
when
our brain looses
rhythm
and
we may very well
shoot
at you in our dark

Seeking shelter in
an old house

hark
the bruise
of mono,
dicots
slicing
through full
soil
sleeps on
my walls
with sunrise
encouragement
and strings
of gray gravity
making
certain I'm
still in
the right place
to hear
my house's
groans
in this late
winter's storm

Speechless

I said to the water
just ate all the
food on my wife's
plate too

swear I heard water
shudder and turn away
just joking I lied
just joking I cried

the lake turned salty
speechless
feel the waves grow
wow grow

M.L.K.

Survival
is waiting to gain more
patience
I know my warm house
cats
sleep in their different
loc-
ations and have to
re-
acquaint, must be
fed
in separate dishes
during
colliding house religions

dry
bread of quarreling
renown
while I was once a
hiker
with all the sharp
edges
biting into my cloudy
family
history yet still the man
of
dissolved prayer though
those
gone do not all think so

wearing

their own rough mantels as

weary

shadows sliding in moon

light

yet angled towards the sun

Pull!

Where have I gone wrong

a song filters through
fog
that covers the field
almost
an answering call
from
the other density

no need for a trap
all
my rifles and guns
are
scattered about. I'm
neither
an angel or butterfly

wrapped
body and all unable to
climb
that noisy white wall
nor
need a trap tripping
PULL

seems
my soul seeks new
clay
vessels one after the
other
as kill rate remains
high

especially
in all this fog
where
dreams age with the
flick of your serenading
wrist

I'll go and return

aye
this is nothing
not
the time for
shallow
seas
as it may be
last
fishing trip I'll
go
and return with
thing
that annoyed me
most

hand over hand
pulled
those shiny
slippery
things from below
until
I got to the old
hook
on a line that
found
bottom of my
treachery
similar to those
dark

little composters
flitting
branch to branch
their
beaks glowing
with
today's meal discovery
incapacitated
human
lonely as anyone
else
I hear Ted Roethke's
my
ears can hear the
birds

when all is still
and
I never knew
how
simple it is
when
all my life's
been
about growing
living
in this small
cocoon
of *fish-time*

My Library

I like that
we
can give rise
to
our own creatures

2
cups of dark
coffee
blank-quiet window
to

stare out- coffee
getting
cold after putting
pesky
cat outside to roam

pick
up quick-setting
lime
on dad's trowel
flicking

it onto dense
words
and in between, care-
ful
not to build too

during a setting
wanting
to start again
pleading

with son to grind
me
more lime next
time
please and thanks

washing
dad's tools with
milky
water till so
shiny

The abated

the abated sun
lies
mottled and cooler
than
days before when
it
frowned and held
me
down with liquid
hands

not that it's
that
much cooler
but
memory of a
cooler
time had flown
or
held down in sweaty
hands

so today's sunday
marks
another changing
time
as my last summer's
taut

tether shrinks and
crackles
both ends frayed
loose

Still waiting

My soul is an enchanted
boat -PB Shelley

Oh my soul,
are
you really mine
mother
reverberated
through
a dream as she
was
upset mostly
with
me and I laid
there
wondering where
it
was by running
my
hands over this
lengthening
body of mine
prompted
I was sure by my
soul
but now I hear
that
it isn't even mine

going
from body to
body,
bling from eons
ago,
falling as a drop
into
times internet

What's up with us

maintaining
what else can I
say
about this life of
fear
lust caught in a
vision
of my spiderweb
of
words and narrowly
missed
visions of what I
was
thinking or you
were
thinking bad thoughts
and
my pencil un-grounded
unable
to provide in our neighbors
sense
where our birth right of
vanishing
stars scramble away un-
tidely
in our defenseless wails
so that all there is is
maintaining

and hope with you

insisting

the un- leveled fridge

needs

replacing or what was the

name

of the little boy coming

to

breakfast with our daughters

before

walking to the school-

bus

Babel

how best to send
our
reconstructed dream
bodies
into space where a
biome
does not exist yet

support
is slow and risky
sacrifice
may be necessary
with
change of plans
again

we
should choose to
send
our robots if
they
can be programmed
to

create a welcoming
place
for the wealthiest
leaders

to follow and institute
banks
hoping, hoping

their mechanized
ones
have not by now created
their
own speech binaries
poems
gleefully discarding

bankers into fattening
pens
for later companionship
amid
terrified complaints
now
in our solar system

Dash

we walked the tracks
heading
home after eating
our
runaway sandwiches
made
by our mother that
morning

it had rained all day
so
we found ourselves
on
the wet between rail
lines
hoping we would
hear

whatever it was coming
our
way and we could
scramble
to safety always with
an
eye out of the danger
zone

if we could as I
would
have too also in later
years
frequenting many
museums
in my career as
art

critic floundering in
the wet
between heavy lines
bordering
each other listening
for
danger needing traction
again

Ping

did I really

hear

the trees in

our

town are gone

they

have disappeared

to

another big sky

way

from here and

now

we can not

see

beautiful, spent elm

leaves

rushing to our

feet

nor can we feel

you

way out in bright

opaque

country where no

one

hides in piles of

desiccation

Begging for time

while the earth
decides
what to do with
it

truly sorry that
I
do not know what
day

it is, all I can
remember
is that I started
reading

in the beginning of
August
while the dry lawn,
flowers

were beginning their
nose
dive into fall
roots

then the earth
decided
what to do with
itself

Tumult

with the first
light
the debris of
angry
words between
slith-
ering commas
for
those too poor
to
evacuate when
told
while too late
horses,
assateague's
finest,
calm as their
last
barrier is breached
and
you who stayed
scream
to wildly rocking
Noah's
help me, help
me
and my kittens

Early morning

Now we will
have
no bread for our
toast
how clear their
call
feeding Ravens
on
a foggy morning,
Vapah
it is sometimes
thought
of, as it hides
usual's
from our view
which
we peer, strain
to
re see and yet the
clacks
of reason rings
clear
in compelling
void
where dust-like
shadows
fly about in solid
wind

Chanticleer

the pause, intuitive
knowledge,
is fitting up as the
winter's
chores were finished

and this morning's
slight
rain has drawn me
to
favorite Maples

some leaves still
green
while others thank-
full
for the changing

relief from heavy
color,
onto stiff shoes already
bitten
by frost's smooth hands

wary too in wind
Red
may crow early as always
never
letting on what today

will bring for fit forage
while
we were settled for the
night
still distracted by colors

Call of the void

Diesel drone under
hardening
bark
this isn't wind song
from
maples but a growl
at
winter's impending
stranding
octave of white fury

so it is that I have
come
to understand why
you
left at this time last
year
raking those leaves
you
loved to touch so
much

those leaves of spring
summer
and fall are gone now
wind's
shriller now but still
throbbing

under the bark that
holds
me tight asking fore-
giveness

Once

Waiting for night's calm
where
hiding from myself is
easier
this is where my
journey
turns liquid wrapped in
sail
to ward off the rest of
Orca's
light reflecting sunlight
in
the dark sea waves that
over-
whelm my restricted
strokes
and the play-prey
lying
about friendship's toothy
grin
or how she would love
to
undress me into the
moon-
light, splash herself
across
this watery table-bed
devour

my luscious, scarred
liver
and I can only clutch my
sail
tighter around my neck
sinking
below this rising dream

Kestrel mania

she hovers to think
dives down into a
slow thought I was
remembering as
my genes predicted

now her mouth opens
to yell at me and
the thought as she
pitches down with
deadly claws

grabbing that evasive
struggling thing brings
it back to her staging-
where you know the rest-
bones will litter the ground

Omnivorous

"And then went down to the ship,
Set keel to breakers, forth on the godly sea, and
We set up mast and sail on that swart ship. - E Pound

those shackles festering

beneath

the waves lie motionless

in

the long night and now

begin

to change color as a

sanguine

sea urge rolls on, on

metals

last ditch attempt for

freedom

after all hands on deck

was

caught in the wind that

rolled

against an astonished

wall

of impervious stone as

surfaces

of the world that bear

beloved

citizens on their way

Wild things

who else listens
noises
outside dark win-
dows

I strike a balance
with
aching feet- please
allow

me to go outside
chase
down barefoot
as

I did a fox who
swiped
a chicken off the
roost

until he dropped her
as
I gained on him
found
checked
for damage only
were
two holes in neck

so I put her back on
roost
to check in morning
she

strutted after corn
on
the worn ground's
tightness

perhaps if I could
I
would find another
egg

layer in this darkness
even
though none are raised
here
any more any more

Uneasy rest

a crown on my ghost
child
crawling through
neurons

downward spiral of
memory
my last book lies
where

fluttering pages
hold
where the very
edge

erodes and no one
can
recover from our
evolving

wee creatures on
earth
do not just live and
die

without changing the
landscape
rest easy my ghost

child

Fantasy

I still like to imagine
as
I did when young
though
I don't shut my eyes
so
forcibly now but the
stars
go away as I stand on the
lawn
close them and life, space
con-
sciousness obliterates any
knowledge:
time, space even cosmos
and
I am alone in fright of
what
to do next, thankfully
voices
collide on wind- pineal
strain-
Noah has already gone
and
I feel rain on my fore-
head
opening my eyes to the
stars

Doctor

I kept asking that
doctor

who wanted to
snip
part of a band in
my
DNA spiral to ease
my
life in its latter
stages
why did he think

that
my childhood, any
child-
hood, would be our
only
origin as the DNA "s
probably
my soul that I
share

with more than
I
could possibly know
as
quite probably on

death
this soul flies to
a
cloud then collected

by
someone who selects
best
samples for a glowing
child
swimming with eyes
closed
needing this push of
life

I see

it all now how my
kitch
primitive, intuitive
opens

in this slightly
humid
air and when it's
pages

were opened flutt-
ered
briefly as if re-
sponding

to a memory
chirality,
protein molecule

be
the left side of
mirror

go past the
house
where we were
borne

no one will
notice
our ancestral
wings

Absorbing trees

glint of re-
flecting
moon on your
knitted
bark sings to
you
of the many
notes
in flowing root
water

wind
many silent
shades
of green bouncing
assuring
tides that broken
limbs
are not loneliness
best
bodies gripping
bedrock
enjoy being afloat

soon
way too soon
those
saline

seas will return
and
our litter grind
in
slip faults
churned
earth your rings
left
to tell the tale

of
fat feeder birds
scurry
back to their
woods

Terraforme

silacious dust blows
across
as our planet's cross
winds
grow the footless
sculpted
wings unseen by
pilots
and passengers
strapped
tightly against the
initial
thudding of takeoff
or
mind-change that
had
so many previous
passengers
looking out and muttering
My God
this looks so much
like
where we are going to
die

Solstice with
full moon

that
we are no
longer
afraid during
solstices
among these
trees
now shadows
are
mere dreams
had
of how coffee
stains
and rings would
make
and record
how
I tried to make
myself
nightly in this
world
of continuing
night
where a certain
serpentine
request and apple
made

sense again and
I
should make
that
call to you

Bowl

they never knew
whose
been sitting on
an
inverted hollowed
burl
silently listening
decibels
of dust settling
with
our own arrogant
voices-
time to depart
chimes
and sighs of new
extinction
from everywhere
while
sleep's a forgotten
thing
for some with
their
dainty garlands
we
placed on our de-
fenders-
altered in war
zones-

with smaller comfort
for
coming back too
soon

Flammable

I find myself
finally
on the Three
Hundred
Sixty-Fifth day
grown
beyond that
old
Proverb: With
the old
almanac and the
old
year, Leave thy
old
vices though
ever
so dear, as
I have lived beyond
my
vices and couldn't
even
if I dared to
give
credence to those
supposedly
lottery-pics wondering
what

will fail next in

glorious

New Years advent

A day

It was cold, the
new
year had begun
when
our dog said
good-
bye and we
wander-
ed strange woods tool-
less
with himself for a
pyre
above the frozen
granite
that even I couldn't
budge
returning alone I
heard
it and watched the
murder
land in a near by
tree
then descend knowing
what
those branches could
not
do was accomplished
and

I thanked sanguine
snow,
red beaks plus the
fox
on its way in the
clear
sunshine continuing

Good bye

now the lights
stay
on I dreamed of
Ravens
every night I
was
gone causing
us
to stir in their
night
as if a wind,
my
dream, floated
over
them in darkness

how silly they
acted
while I cast
stale
bread as I spoke
to
them in my non
native
Raven causing
quiet
while attempting
translation
yet it was the

bread
that
mattered in a
dream
gone sunshine and
bare
branches with
me
so far away
forever
drowning in withdrawal's
power

Nepantia

today I got
an
early start before
dew
dissipation on
Hoodoo
caps still de-
ploring
the noise you
make
me make crushing
those
beauties cautiously
freed
freed wind at its
end
disappearing in
dust
covering my dumb
bulldozer's
surrounding dry-land
scape
while a mining CEO
hovering
the far East Coast
keeps
asking if we
are
done yet, done
yet

Exaptation

I seem to
have
spent all my
time
filling shoes
to
an impossible
size
and now have
no
dreams that
glitter
and scold for
I
have grown
older
in a landscape
that
silences water
with
sand a hand-
full
at a time
just
to hear that
hiss
of dryness
yes

I remember
doing
that once and
father
admonishing
said
what a mess
you
have made
muddy
mess you should
know
better go in
wash
those dirty hands

Vague paths

you're thinking
about
forgiveness as you
attempt
to change Ptolemies
map
etched so long ago

who would have
thought
that these modern
Hebrews
would turn their
nation
parabalani-

monks
serving as henchmen
splitting
children legs with
your
well oiled boots
while

snow swirls while
I
choose modification
comfort

while life grows
jaded
thinking I have so much

Midnight meander

imaginary #1
and
initial singularity
forever
waiting, wanting
transition
out of nothing
as I
relieved the weight
of my
mother who picked
me up
fed me and saw that I
expanded:
burst of light
through
the window in such
darkness
of night and then
cold
wind entering the
forest
she thought no one
would
believe and we never
spoke
of it again until
now

she's gone and I
might
be anytime soon
as
the fire thins no
longer
reflecting in the
window
drawing me back
from
illusion with flair
conviction

Aural

To the scribe of the Infinite
Of the words it had to write
Because they were past its ken."
- Thomas Hardy

my tumbledown words
hacked
from the ancestral
mountain
welded to me in a
town
of the same name:
recipes
that express feeling
extend
all the way to outer
space
oral arms stretched
maybe
beyond as conscious
beings
that existed before
the
big bang and slowly
drifted
back to me to see
if
I know what aural's

talking
about in the dim
light
of morning's pre-
dawn
and I am waking
from
dreams that taunt me
slowly
slowly into another
day

Back

stand
something special
but
no longer an impulse
yet
still braving myself
into
the darkest of this
night
where the conscious
words
lie tangled, feeling for
ones
to extract slowly
amassing
as we all slide:
both
back into the times
before
that big bang inter-
rupted
snowfalls of bending
regret
borrowed words
worlds
that stand apart worlds
apart
bodily pain strewn

our
only light
light

Happening as happenstance

Xsquared x Ysquared =1
cheeks already
dark
minstrel man
feet
traveling boards
in
big, dark fields
circling
big, dark trees
rung
round with dis-
ease
smiling breathlessly
this
is great comedy
slap
struck through
life
Xsquared xYsquared= circle
peeled
from mirror to
mirror

Re entry

unique as the how's of
sanity
when our/my universe
has
gone from singularity
to
singularity prior to
exploding
again
towards another re-
menbrance
wishing for some reason
hope
that there will be
remnants
of our serene floating
around
in clouds of Wordsworthian
glory
or become a point again
pointless
waiting statistically
comfort-
able as non significant
ergo
as shadows follow a
child
standing on one foot

Anon

what is with all
this
forgetting things
before
the white wall
nearest
the bad flowered
beautiful
birds something
seen
read with the strum
of
tears then forgetting
revel
in pain becoming
exotic
in the all but
nor
would I turn down
this
night's cast waves
as
against my will
frost
comes so quickly
paining
one who remembered
every
thing

Alive, oh

I live in old
derelict
buildings I am one
listen
to all the sighs
before
the roof caves
scramble
out to the grown
yard
yelling forgive
them
they know not
they
do know forgive
me
I know that they
do
and why but I have
added
your sighs to mine
admit
the snapping of
timber

Freedom

uncommon too
preoccupied
myself tugged by
rip

I was astounded
by
the size of that
hook

I did get the
damn
thing worrying
losing

a hand or arm
from
reflex action
as

I had to open his
mouth
to pull the steely
thing

through and past
those
amazing teeth plus
I

saw a flicker of an
eye
imagined or not
as

I worked the barb
free
and then we were
free

again as if he'd
beached
out on a wave
indifferent

we littorally
swam
not knowing
which

way was up
and
yet when motion
stopped

he thought now
I'm
anonymous for
sure

now is my chance
to yell
help I'm here
help

www.ingramcontent.com/pod-product-compliance
Lightning Source LLC
LaVergne TN
LVHW011211080426
835508LV00007B/726